WEEKLY WR READER®
EARLY LEARNING LIBRARY

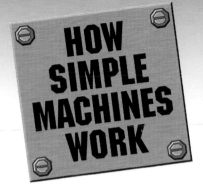

HOW SIMPLE MACHINES WORK

HOW WHEELS AND AXLES WORK

by **Jim Mezzanotte**
Reading consultant: Susan Nations, M.Ed.,
author/literacy coach/consultant
Science and curriculum consultant: Debra Voege, M.A.,
science and math curriculum resource teacher

Please visit our web site at: www.garethstevens.com
For a free color catalog describing Weekly Reader® Early Learning Library's list
of high-quality books, call 1-877-445-5824 (USA) or 1-800-387-3178 (Canada).
Weekly Reader® Early Learning Library's fax: (414) 336-0164.

Library of Congress Cataloging-in-Publication Data

Mezzanotte, Jim.
    How wheels and axles work / by Jim Mezzanotte.
       p. cm. — (How simple machines work)
    Includes bibliographical references and index.
    ISBN-10: 0-8368-7350-5 — ISBN-13: 978-0-8368-7350-4 (lib. bdg.)
    ISBN-10: 0-8368-7355-6 — ISBN-13: 978-0-8368-7355-9 (softcover)
    1. Simple machines—Juvenile literature. 2. Wheels—Juvenile literature.
  3. Axles—Juvenile literature. I. Title. II. Series: Mezzanotte, Jim.
  How simple machines work.
  TJ147.M494   2006
  621.8—dc22   2006008670

This edition first published in 2007 by
Weekly Reader® Early Learning Library
A Member of the WRC Media Family of Companies
330 West Olive Street, Suite 100
Milwaukee, WI 53212 USA

Managing editor: Mark J. Sachner
Art direction: Tammy West
Cover design, page layout, and illustrations: Dave Kowalski
Photo research: Sabrina Crewe

Picture credits: Cover, title © Alan Schein/CORBIS; p. 5 © David Young-Wolff/PhotoEdit;
p. 6 © Jeff Greenberg/PhotoEdit; p. 9 © Amy Etra/PhotoEdit; p. 10 © David Stoecklein/
CORBIS; p. 11 © Bonnie Kamin/PhotoEdit; p. 13 © Tony Freeman/PhotoEdit;
p. 15 © Davis Barber/PhotoEdit; p. 17 © Photo Collection Alexander Alland, Sr./CORBIS;
pp. 18, 21 © Royalty-Free/CORBIS; p. 19 © Neil Rabinowitz/CORBIS; p. 20 © Tom
Stewart/CORBIS

Printed in the United States of America

1 2 3 4 5 6 7 8 9 10 09 08 07 06

TABLE OF CONTENTS

Cover and title page: Ferris wheels and carousels are simple machines that use a wheel and axle to produce motion — and fun!

CHAPTER 1

THE WORLD OF WHEELS

Wheels are everywhere. They are on cars and trucks, trains and planes. Skateboards have wheels. So do bikes, wagons, strollers, and scooters.

Rolling wheels help people and things get around. But wheels help with other jobs, too. A doorknob is a wheel. So are the handles of a faucet. The handle of a screwdriver is a wheel. A clock has wheels with teeth, called **gears**.

This skateboard travels quickly on its wheels.

The bus driver steers by using a wheel.

A spinning CD is also a wheel. You steer a car with a wheel. A pencil sharpener is a wheel with a handle. Can you spot any wheels around you?

CHAPTER 2

HOW WHEELS WORK

Today, a lot of machines are complicated. But they often have many **simple machines** working together.

The wheel and axle is a simple machine. It lets you do a lot of work without a lot of effort. In this case, "work" just means moving something.

A wheel usually has an **axle**. An axle is a shaft in the wheel's center. Some wheels turn with the axle. Doorknobs work this way.

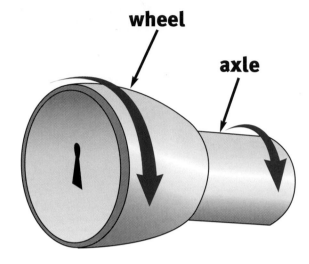

wheel

axle

Other wheels spin around the axle, and the axle doesn't move. Wheels on a wagon may work this way.

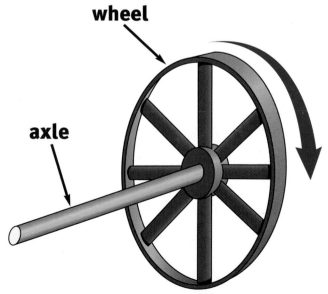

wheel

axle

A wagon makes it easy to move things and people.

Have you ever dragged a heavy box? It is a hard job! The box rubs on the floor, creating **friction**. Friction is what keeps things from moving smoothly against each other. If you pull the box in a wagon, the job is much easier. Only small parts of the wheels ever touch the floor. There is much less friction. Large wheels roll easier than small wheels.

Leg power makes these bikes move.

A wheel needs power to turn. If you ride a bike, the power comes from your legs. In a car, the power comes from an engine. This power turns the axle, which then turns the wheel.

Other wheels work differently. When you turn a doorknob, you turn the outside of the wheel. The wheel then turns the axle. Steering wheels and screwdrivers work this way, too.

By turning a doorknob, you turn its axle.

CHAPTER 3

KINDS OF WHEELS

Some wheels have a handle on them. This handle is called a **crank**. With a crank, you can turn a wheel's axle. The handle of a pencil sharpener is a crank. So are the pedals of a bike. Cranks may be used to wind ropes or lines. A fishing pole has a crank. You use it to reel in a fish on the line.

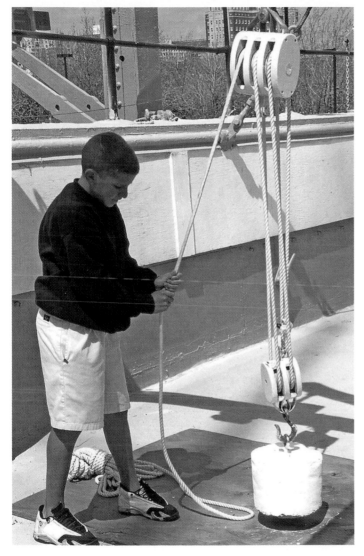

A **pulley** is a wheel with a groove. A rope fits in the groove. As you pull the rope, the wheel turns. Using a pulley, you can lift or move heavy things.

This boy is using pulleys to help him lift.

Gears are wheels with teeth. Their teeth mesh, or fit into each other. One gear can then turn another gear. It turns the other gear in the opposite direction. Different-sized gears turn at different speeds. So, gears can change how quickly something spins, and in what direction it spins, too.

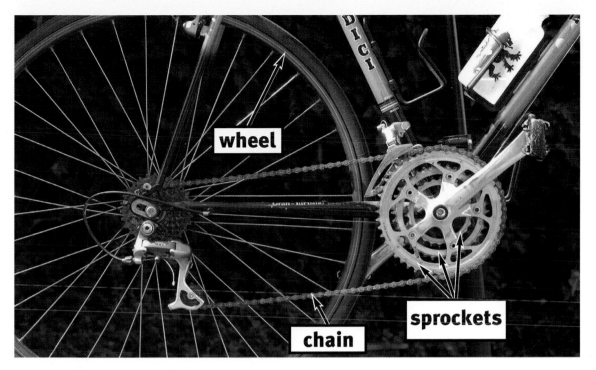

A bike has sprockets. Teeth on the sprockets grab
hold of the chain and help the rear wheel turn.

A car's **transmission** has many gears. They change the
car's pulling power and its speed. Bikes have gears called
sprockets. These gears have teeth that catch the bike's chain.
As the rider pedals and turns the sprocket, the chain turns
the rear wheel.

CHAPTER 4

WHEELS IN HISTORY

The wheel has been around for more than five thousand years. Ancient people in many parts of the world used it. No one is sure who first invented the wheel.

This old-fashioned cart has wooden wheels with spokes.

Early carts were just boxes with wheels. Animals such as horses could pull the carts. At first, wheels were solid wood. Later, wheels had **hubs** and **spokes**. These wheels weighed less than solid wood wheels. They made carts easier to pull.

By the 1800s, steam trains rolled on metal wheels.
Steamships used paddle wheels instead of sails.

A big paddle wheel makes this steamboat move.

Tires help cars ride smoothly over bumps.

Cars came along in the 1900s. After a while, their wheels had rubber tires. The tires were filled with air. With rubber tires, cars had smoother rides.

This girl is using a potter's wheel to shape a clay pot.

Through the years, people have used wheels for many jobs. Ancient people used them to grind food and shape pottery. Later, people used them to spin yarn. People built wheels to pump water and provide power. These wheels were turned by wind or rushing water. Some people use wheelchairs to help them get around. Wheels are still used to steer cars and boats.

Today, there are new jobs for wheels. A computer has a wheel called a hard drive. This wheel is a **disc** that holds information. As the disc spins, the computer reads the information. Who knows what tomorrow's wheels will be?

A computer has a spinning disc, called a hard drive.

GLOSSARY

axle: the shaft at the center of a wheel. A wheel can spin around an axle, or it can spin with the axle.

crank: a handle that attaches to a wheel and is used to turn the wheel

disc: a flat, circular object

friction: anything that keeps two surfaces from moving against each other easily

gears: wheels with teeth that mesh, or fit into each other. When two gears mesh, one gear can turn the other gear.

hubs: the centers of wheels that have spokes. The axle is in the center of the hub, and the spokes go from the hub to the wheel's outer ring, called the rim.

pulley: anything that a line can move around. The line is usually a rope or cable. The pulley is usually a wheel with a groove for the line. As you pull on the line, it moves on the turning pulley. Pulleys make it easier to move things.

simple machines: devices with few or no moving parts. They let you do a lot of work without a lot of effort.

spokes: strong bars that go from a wheel's outer rim to its inner hub. A wheel with spokes is usually lighter than a solid wheel.

sprockets: gears that turn chains instead of other gears. Bikes and most motorcycles have chains and sprockets.

transmission: the part of a car that takes the engine's spinning power and sends it to the wheels. With its many gears, it can change the speed of a car.

22

INDEX

About the Author

Jim Mezzanotte has written many books for children. He lives in Milwaukee with his wife and two sons. He uses simple machines every day.

FOR MORE INFORMATION

BOOKS

Sensational Science Projects with Simple Machines. Fantastic Physical Science Experiments (series). Robert Gardner (Enslow Publishers)

Wheels and Axles. Early Bird Physics (series). Sally M. Walker and Roseann Feldmann (Lerner Publications)

Wheels and Cranks. Machines in Action (series). Angela Royston (Heinemann)

WEB SITES

Edheads: Simple Machines
edheads.org/activities/simple-machines/
At this interactive site, you can learn all about simple machines, including pulleys.

Mikids.com: Simple Machines
www.mikids.com/Smachines.htm
This site has examples of simple machines, including pulleys. It also has fun activities to help you learn more about simple machines.